Solos & Duets for Snare Drum

By Louie Bellson

Alfred's
PERCUSSION
PERFORMANCE SERIES

Preface

In the fall of 2008, I met with Louie Bellson to go over some new pieces he had written. Among the items he showed me were four new snare drum pieces (three solos and one duet). Rather than publish them individually, I thought they would work better as part of a collection. Towards that end, I asked Louie if he would be willing to write some additional solos to round out the collection. Unfortunately, he passed away several months later and those additional solos were never written.

As a tribute to Louie, I was determined to publish those last few pieces but still felt they would work better as a collection. As luck would have it, I discovered some additional solos and duets he had written many years prior and was happy to find they worked well with the four new solos he showed me that fall afternoon.

Alfred is proud to offer this collection of solos and duets by the late Louie Bellson, which includes the last few snare drum solos he ever wrote.

Dave Black

Dave Black
Vice President and Editor-in-Chief,
School and Church Publishing

Table of Contents

Chicken in the Basket

Louie Bellson

This solo is based on the melody *Turkey in the Straw*. The melody goes along with the drum part at (A). (B) is a drum-solo interlude. (C) is a variation against the melody, and (D) is the Finale as a drum solo.

Beat High, Beat Low

Louie Bellson

In this solo, special attention must be given to the dynamics throughout. The correct effect and performance depends upon a musical interpretation of all markings.

Flight of the Wild Goose

Louie Bellson

The effect of this solo is largely dependent upon a proper interpretation of all dynamics.

Out on a Wing

Louie Bellson

This solo must be clear and crisp. Carefully observe (at letter C) the single, double, triple and quadruple development of the sticking.

Spitfire Syncopation

Louie Bellson

Stick Kicks

Louie Bellson

In this solo, there are many single and double strokes which are to be played in the open position.

Trixie

(Right foot on the floor included.)

Louie Bellson

This solo is based on the melody *Dixie*, and includes a "trick" foot beat, which is introduced at (B). The effect is produced by stomping the foot on the floor, which is indicated by the bass drum beats.

(for Andy Weis)

Louie Bellson

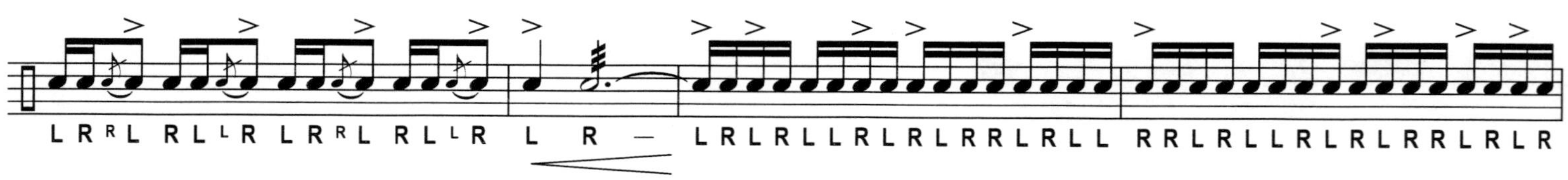

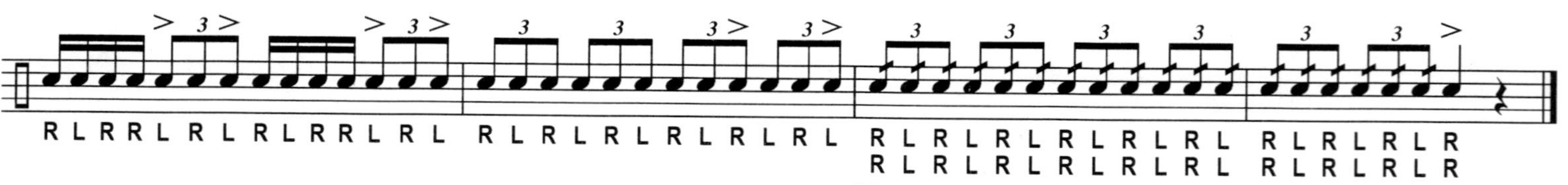

Turn Terry Loose

Louie Bellson

Yin and Yang

Louie Bellson

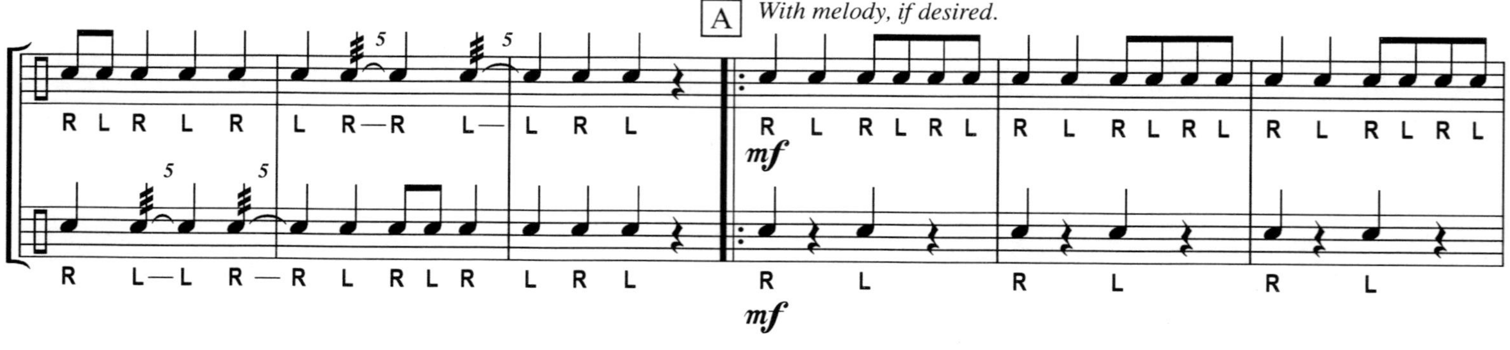

Refinement is the key to an overall musician-like rendition in this duet, which may be played against the tune *American Patrol*. It is suggested that the head of the stick be played on the drum head, and that the rim shot is produced with the other stick against it.

C With melody
D Finale

Two for the Road

(Right foot on the floor included.)

Louie Bellson

This duet includes a "trick" foot beat. The effect is produced by stomping the foot on the floor, which is indicated by the bass drum beats.

D
f
f
E
ff
ff

Double Up

Louie Bellson

This is an exciting duet, and each soloist must interpret their part so the composite picture is dainty and musical.

C
staccato
p
mf
staccato
sfz
13
D
mf
E
f
pp
ff
p

Sticks of a Kind

Louie Bellson

This drum duet may be played against the first strain of the *National Emblem March* and half of the second strain. It is an original duet, of course, and does not need the melody.

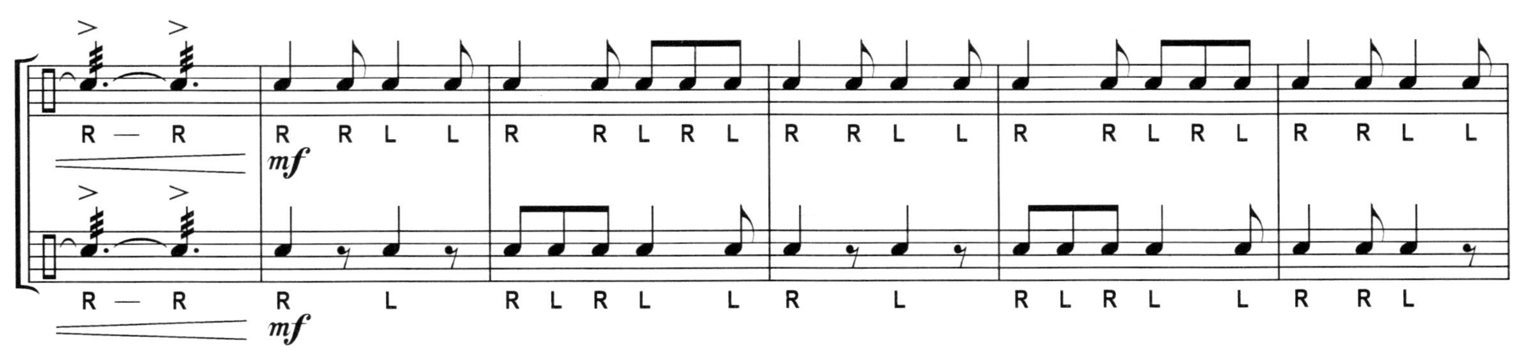
R — R R R L L R R L R L R R L L R R L R L R R L L
mf
R — R R L R L R L L R L R L R L L R R L
mf

R R — R — R — R — R R R L L R R L R L R R L L
pp mf
R R — R — R — R — R R L R L R L L R L
pp mf

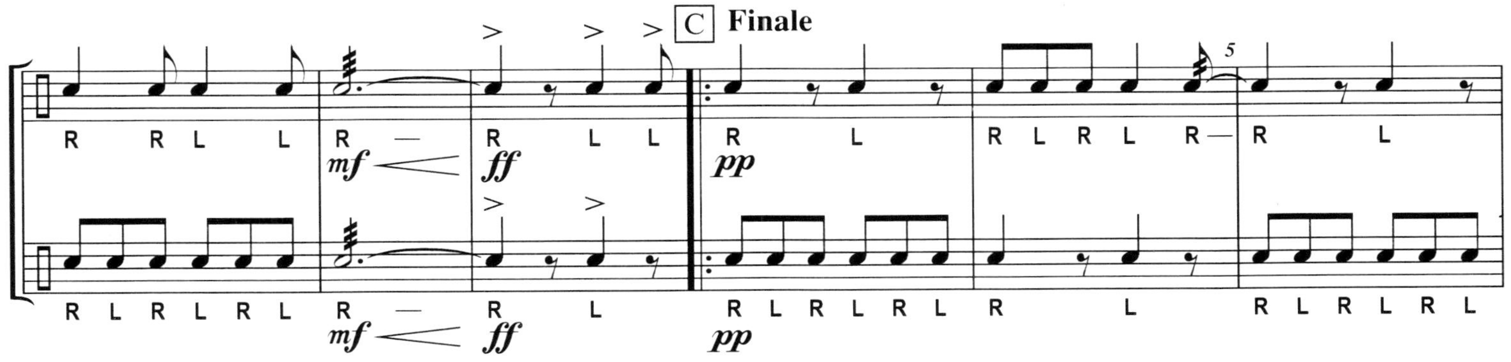
C Finale
5
R R L L R — R L L R L R L R L R — R L
mf ff pp
R L R L R L R — R L R L R L R L R L R L R L R L
mf ff pp

5
R L R L R — R L R R L R L R L R L R L R R L R L R L R L
5 5
R L R L — L R — R L R L R L R L R L R L R L

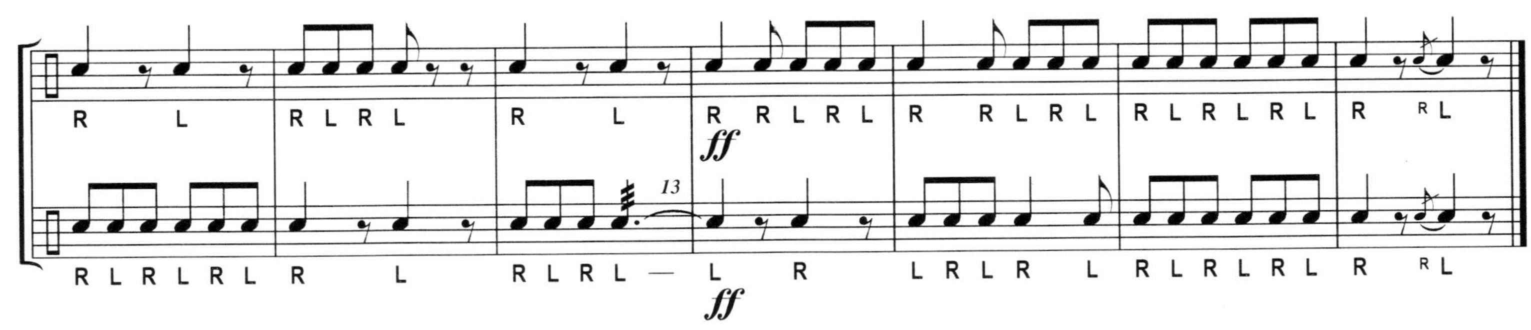
R L R L R L R L R R L R L R R L R L R L R L R L R RL
ff
13
R L R L R L R L R L R L — L R L R L R L R L R L R L R RL
ff

Two of Us

In this duet, carefully observe the differences in dynamics required of the soloist. At (A), the first part is ***mf***, while the second part is ***p***.

C
D